CATTLE DRIVE!

BOOK THREE OF THE GROVEHILL GANG SERIES

Written and illustrated by Jacqueline Ward

FOGBOUND BOOKS

Vancouver Island, BC

National Library of Canada Cataloguing in Publication Data

Ward, Jacqueline, 1947-
Cattle drive!

(The Grovehill gang ; bk. 3)
ISBN 0-9686693-2-8

I. Title. II. Series: Ward, Jacqueline, 1947- . Grovehill gang ; bk. 3.

PS8595.A736C38 2001 jC813'.6 C2001-900224-6
PZ7.W2126Ca 2001

Published by
FOGBOUND BOOKS
640 Grovehill Road
Qualicum Beach, BC V9K 2A3
250-757-9571
www.thegrovehillgang.com

Page design by Jean Robinson
Printed in Canada by Friesens

Shiloh & Stetson

Blaze

Repo & Jake

Dear Readers,

Welcome to *Cattle Drive!*, the third book in 'The Grovehill Gang' series of farm stories about us—some real live animals who live on Grovehill Farm.

Just like the first two books, this story is based on things that really happened. Have you ever had a horse? Well, if you have, you will know that they are not very brave. *Cattle Drive!* tells about the day Stetson, Shiloh and Blaze helped to herd the cows down the road.

Don't forget—the line on the bottom of every page is especially written for beginning readers. If you can read, you might like to share this book with a younger buddy.

We hope you'll enjoy finding out just how silly our horses can be.

Happy reading!

Sprout

PigPig

Keeper

Wrangler the Bull

Spring was back and the horses on Grovehill Farm were tickled pink. Good-bye snow and cold! Hello sunshine and green grass!

But something was worrying Blaze."Hey Shiloh," he said as he munched on the new pasture, "what's a Cattle Drive?"

Shiloh looked puzzled. "I don't know. Maybe it means the cows go somewhere in the truck. Why?"

"Well," answered Blaze. "PigPig told me she heard Farmer Mom and Farmer Dad talking about you and me and Stetson going on a Cattle Drive."

The horses loved spring.

Shiloh frowned. A Cattle Drive sounded like work to him and all he really wanted to do was lounge around and be a pasture potato!

"Hey Stetson, what's a Cattle Drive?" Blaze asked when his friend the big black horse galloped over.

"I don't know. Maybe it means the cows learn to drive!" Stetson laughed. He flicked his tail, kicked up his heels and thundered away in a burst of spring energy.

The happy black horse ran off.

The next morning Farmer Mom came to the barn with her friends. As they brushed the horses, they joked and laughed. As they cleaned the hooves, they talked about how brave and useful horses were. As they tightened up the saddles, they chatted about how awesome the First Annual Grovehill Road Cattle Drive was going to be.

Stetson and Shiloh and Blaze just looked at each other. They *still* didn't know what was going on.

At the barn the horses got ready for a ride.

Grovehill Farm

When the riders were ready and up in the saddle, off they all went down the driveway. Stetson was in the lead because he is The Boss. Then came Blaze, and finally Shiloh who would just as soon stay at home anyway.

“We may not know what a Cattle Drive is,” said Stetson, “but what a grand day for a ride! We’re headed off on our same old road, so I don’t think there will be any bad surprises in store for us.”

Off they all went for their ride.

Meanwhile, down the road a way, another family was getting ready for the Cattle Drive. They herded Sarah the cow and her little calf Suzie into a pen. They put up ropes to keep Sarah and Suzie on the right path. They filled a bucket with grain and placed it on the back of the ATV.

"This is going to be fun!" said Farmer John to his wife. "All we have to do is get Sarah up the road to Grovehill Farm to spend some time with Wrangler the Bull. This should be an easy Cattle Drive. I'll go in front with the grain bucket and Sarah and Suzie will follow me.The horses can just trot along behind to keep the cow and calf moving. Come on Holly Dog. You can help too!"

The cows needed to go to another farm.

It wasn't long before Stetson and Shiloh and Blaze arrived in Farmer John's field. Stetson checked out the situation and relaxed. Sheep munched quietly in the next field. A cow and calf stood watching from a nearby pen. Farmer John and his family leaned against their ATV at the end of the drive.

"Nothing unusual going on here," said The Boss and he put his nose down into the fresh spring grass.

When Shiloh and Blaze saw that everything was okay, they too relaxed and started to graze. This was just the kind of day Shiloh loved best—standing around eating!

"Oh look, it's just some cows," said Stetson.

Then quick as lightning everything changed!

Farmer John opened the gate to the pen. Sarah and Suzie trotted into the field and looked around for the best way out. The horses threw up their heads and exclaimed in one voice *"Yikes! There are cows in here with us!"*

Stetson snorted! Shiloh bucked! Blaze pranced!

Around they went in circles, stirring up the ground and banging into each other.

The horses went wild!

"Get those cattle out onto the road!" hollered Farmer Mom. "We'll be fine once we're headed in the right direction!"

Farmer John started his ATV and gave the grain bucket a shake. Sarah's head shot up and her eyes went wide. Grain! Yum! She galloped after the grain bucket with Suzie tagging along as best she could.

The cows saw a treat they wanted.

SARAH'S GRAIN

Finally, the ATV was out on the road.

Holly Dog and all the helpers were out on the road.

Sarah and Suzie were out on the road.

The Cattle Drive was on!

Everyone was ready to go.

SARAH'S
GRAIN
6X6 POLARIS

But it was just too-o-o-o much for the horses.

"Why are there cows on the road?" Blaze yelled as he panicked backward down into the ditch.

"There are <u>never</u> cows on this road!" shouted Shiloh as he leaped straight up into the air.

"This is really very weird!" cried Stetson as he tried to look cool and in charge, but he scrambled backwards until he too was in the ditch with Blaze.

All the horses were very upset.

CHRISTOPHER
HEIDI

And all three horses bucked and jigged and tossed their heads. They kicked up dust and spun in circles. Round and round they went while the riders just hung on.

"No way there should be cows on this road!"
yelled Blaze.

"There are <u>never</u> cows outside a fence!"
Shiloh shouted.

"This is really, <u>really</u>, <u>REALLY</u> very weird!"
cried Stetson.

The horses were absolutely sure this was the scariest moment of their lives!

They didn't listen to the riders even one little bit.

YAHOO!!
RIDE 'EM, COWGIRL!

Finally, when Sarah, Suzie and the ATV were so far down the road that they were almost out of sight, Farmer Mom and her friends managed to get the horses quiet.

"Wow! That was pretty scary!" shivered Blaze. "That was a really close call! Good thing those cows ran away from us! I bet they were as scared as we were."

"Well," scoffed Stetson after a while, "*I* wasn't really scared, just a little surprised, that's all." He tried his best to look as calm as a Boss should be and not let the others see the sweat glistening on his forehead.

Even the big, brave, black horse had been scared.

When the horses finally arrived at Grovehill Farm, Farmer Dad and Farmer John were on the lawn having coffee. Sarah and Suzie chomped contentedly in the pasture with Wrangler, Mighty Mite and all the other cows.

"Fine help your horses were, Mom!" laughed Farmer Dad. "We'll have to be sure to [illegible] them next time too!"

Blaze's ears perked up. "See guys," he said to Stetson and Shiloh. "We were a great help. Dad said so! There's nothing to this Cattle Drive job."

"I think they needed us," said Blaze.

But Stetson wasn't so sure.

And Shiloh just laughed.

He knew they'd never again be asked along on a Cattle Drive!

And that was the one and only Grovehill Road Cattle Drive!

. . . for all the helpers — Cari, Kati, John, Lesley, Claire, Grant and, of course, Holly Dog . . . jw

OTHER BOOKS IN 'THE GROVEHILL GANG' SERIES

Book One: *The Naughty Seven*
PigPig works herself into a fine state and learns a valuable lesson when she eavesdrops on Farmer Mom and Farmer Dad.

Book Two: *Jake's Lunch*
He's cute. He's cuddly. He's willing to teethe on anything . . . until the day this puppy's appetite leads to a HUGE misadventure.

Coming Next: *Repo's Story*
One little Springer puppy goes merrily off to his new home, only to find it's not what he expected.

Come visit us at www.thegrovehillgang.com